A LICK AND A PROMISE

IMELDA MAY

A LICK AND A PROMISE

FABER *ff* MUSIC

'Quick!' she said
'Have a lick
and a promise'
then ran
out the door
in a flurry.

FOR VIOLET . . .

Never shrink,
Grow!

FOREWORD

Roddy Doyle

I found out that Imelda May was a poet during what became known as the first lockdown. (We didn't know at the time that there'd be a second, and a third.) I'd been walking the same two permitted kilometres for months. I live very near the sea but, as a neighbour said to me one morning, 'I'm fuckin' sick of the sea.' I was sick of the sea, the sky, the seagulls, the anxious faces of the people coming at me; I was sick of my own anxious face. I was living in Dublin but beginning to forget its map, its rhythm and its voices.

But a day came when the permitted 2K became 5, and I could turn and walk in the opposite direction, into the city centre. The streets were quiet and a bit desolate but that was why I noticed the poster.

'You don't get to be racist and Irish'

It was the only new thing I'd seen all day.

It was a poem, simply that, just words on the poster, down the huge page on the wall. It was angry but playful too – exuberant. As I read I felt I was being reacquainted with the city's rhythm; the words on the wall were making up for the emptiness of the streets. I'd read about half the poem before I saw that it had been written by Imelda May. And, really, it didn't surprise me. I could hear Imelda now as I read – the swagger in the accent, the pride, the humour, the honesty and generosity, the brilliance.

Imelda May is brilliant.

It's simple as that – and as complicated. She can sing 'Johnny Got a Boom Boom' effortlessly, but only because she sat down and wrote it. This book confirms the hard work behind the brilliance. This time, we get only the words and what she can do with them. Imelda May has always been a poet.

A brilliant one.

First published by Faber Music Ltd in 2021
Bloomsbury House
74–77 Great Russell Street
London WC1B 3DA

Edited by Lucy Holliday, Head of Pop Publishing/A&R at Faber Music

Creative direction by Imelda May
Art director and assistant editor, Ami Cadillac
Inside, front and back cover illustrations by Deirdre Mulrooney
Graphic design by Tim Varlow
Typography by Hannah Varlow
Typesetting by Hamish Ironside
Printed and bound in Turkey by Imago

Global Management Craig Logan & Meredith Plant at LME

Literary Agent Adrian Sington at Kruger Cowne Rights Management

www.imeldamay.co.uk

ISBN: 0-571-54193-3
EAN: 978-0-571-54193-5

To buy Faber Music publications or to find out about the full range of titles
available please contact your local retailer or Faber Music sales enquiries:
Faber Music Limited, Burnt Mill, Elizabeth Way, Harlow, CM20 2HX, England
Tel: +44 (0) 1279 82 89 82
fabermusic.com

CONTENTS

BREAST

BLOOD

EYE

TEMPLE

BREAST

Home

'What is love?' you ask . . .
my head spins recalling
every song, story, words and
glorious things I ever heard
every cliché rings in my ears
like a bell announcing the birth
of a new day or the death of yesterday
depends on how you hear it
I haven't a clue
so I ask love
'what are you?'
love replies
'can't you feel me? I'm here
I'm the one holding your hand
reminding you not to forget me
I'm the warm feeling in your belly
when you don't know why
I'm the ache to the core
when one someone sways
to the other side of a vibe
I'm the tingle on your skin
when it's touched by the tip
of a thrill you can rely on
the knowing, when your eyes meet eyes
that recognise yours and hold you
loose enough to move freely
but tight enough to never let you fall
I'm the breath you take in
and let all the way out to the end when you're held and
your shoulders drop into arms you flop
that feel like a blanket of truth
and wrap you and soothe you

to the moon you thought was in the sky
I'm the backbone that holds it all together
the vertebrae stacked on top of each other
when it's all gone pear-shaped and wrong
I'm the biting on your lip
keeping it zipped
swallowing words that could wound and rip apart
I'm choosing kindness over being right
I'm the fight in you when you don't know how
the light in you when it's gone right out
I'm life when I'm near
hope without fear
I'm nothing fancy in a world
dripping in gold
but a beautiful jewel
never bought never sold
and when you open your heart
and let me in alone
you'll know who I am
because I feel like Home.'

Stargazer

The pain
when you came
then almost didn't
I drew strength from an oak
that swayed through the pane
waving at me
in my crisis and crying
I breathed its calm
moving me in harmony
like the chord that
connected you and I
I was afraid
but you? You were just busy
turning your head
getting ready to see the stars
not wanting to miss
the unveiling universe
when you my love were the
greatest reveal of all
I gave you life
but because of you
I live it.

Fairytale

I look out my eyes
at a view I thought lies
I'd never find.
Realising love doesn't hurt
fear of losing it does
I surmise that heaven
might well exist, as every
fairytale, myth has
shimmied awake
and stretched its glorious
truth to my world
I weep with joy.
Turns out I can fly
after all!
My heart aches in my chest
with a bliss
I can hardly bare
and a sprinkling of regret
that we'd not met
when we were both iridescent
and had never known
anything other than this.

Carry Me to the Moon

Put me on your back
and carry me to the moon

She's big and bright and beautiful
but I forgot my shoes

Hold me so I don't fall off
I'll nestle to your neck

And breathe in deep
so I can keep
a night I won't forget.

Etta

The sun sneaked its head out
from a volatile sky
and winked at pansy smiles
that got the joke
Etta James sang her soul out
from across the divide
and I danced in my slippers
with a heart of love and hope.

Don't Throw Away 'I Love You'

Don't throw away 'I love you'
as a flippant flick 'Goodbye'
those words have worth
beyond the stars
way past the farthest skies
don't utter them without intent
or feeling every time
for love's a sacred blessing
of the highest of the high.

Too Much Enough

To love someone is to accept
all versions of them
and feel loved enough
to love them that much.

Bless You

My soul pours 'I love you'
and flows through the walls
down the road
along the shore
under your door
to the foot of your bed
from your feet
to your head
and blesses
you a goodnight.

Albatross

I flew with my free
since the day I first felt it
changed as I needed
to dive from a lie.
I roll on the rise
float on a tide and
breathe as the breeze
lends itself to a life.

Solace

Are you my solace
in this brambled world?
is there a nest
for a bird to rest in?
Are you the warm sun
I can raise my face t'ward
and worship without fear
of being scorched?
Are you the moon that a
tide could turn to
when the pull is overwhelming
without fear of drowning
in the dark?
Are you my solitude
in the swarm that surrounds me
the gaze that grounds me
when I'm swept away?
Are you?
Or is this too much to ask?
I'm not seeking a saviour (I know my God)
nor rescue (I'm capable)
nor a home (that's within me)
nor to complete me (I am whole).
Is it too much to wish for
my other
my lover
my one?

Quick Dive

She spread her lithe arms
like wings stretched wide
I witnessed the moment
she soared to a glide
through a dragonfly sky
then vanished
beneath the glass surface.

Horizon

You're the fire to my sky
the soft of a mist
the petal blush flush
of a fluttering kiss
you're the breath of a breeze
on an oven day
a GAA shawl
on a silver night
you're the lilt
on a laugh I gave away
a million times without the magic
the light on Lough Bay
the sky gave it to gaze into
and see its own beauty looking back
you're the feathers spreading
from my fingertips
lifting me higher than I thought
I could rise without my feet leaving ground
the hand holding mine to a better me
you're the journey proceeding
with the ease of a greased-up ship
all sails up gliding to a horizon
that feels like it could be ours.

Under a Winter Sky

The moon is low and yellow
Jack Frost has just moved in
diamond blades below
reflect its stellar twin

The night is still and knowing
eyes watch that I don't see
I stand alone bestowing
a wish to infinity.

Vascular Vortex

I can lay down my body
but my mind shields my core
that longs to
leap run love
beat for something good
the seed of me
believes the sweet
amouricious
whisper lipped kisses
feathertip touches
the look that blushes my cheeks
like a fledgling never flown
a novice, not yet knowing
a woman in the midst of a glow
unaware of pains to come
my soft sacred heart is scarred and marked
from where it bled before
but infantile ideology, careless cardiology
forgetful frivolity, rosy unreality
sees it skip its simple duties
and fall to its fate
oh head on my shoulders
stay awake! And
keep my vascular vortex safe.

Welcome Inn

Romantic love
is not without equal
all love is worthy
all love needed.
Wipe your feet well
and come in.

I Know How Your Hair Feels

I know how
your hair feels
under my hand
how soft your cheek is

I know how
you breathe as you sleep
as your puffed eyes
flicker a dream

I know how
I love you
wherever I am
wherever you are
infinitely
forever.

The Dancer and the Dream

As the dreamer
gave up the dance
to feed mouths
sat on his shoulders
so the dancer
gave up the dream
and he worked
all day in the cold
normalcy, banter, craic
confined him to 'one of the boys'
he laughed
so as not to stand out
though his stance
polished and poised
innuendos flew
in a man's man's world
in which he could never recline from
the butt of the joke
never drank, swore or smoked
but I swear had
skin of a rhino
once soft hands
stripped by thinners
cracked as the
crust of bread
he was winning
guiding the brush
gripping the ladder
closed position
teacher to partner
tails and tux
buried under coats

that sometimes
doubled as blankets
as Guilded certificates
gleamed in the light
of the telly
that worked
when you banged it
little ones fed
and tucked up in bed
the clowner
became a king
and waltzed downstairs
with his queen
the dancer who
taught us to dream.

*My parents, Tony and
Madge Clabby, on
their first dance*

Hero

Passing moment
day repeated
wasting time
never wasted
beguiled child
'I spy'ing the sky
and suddenly
from an apple
to an eye
you've become
my hero.

BLOOD

Liberty Belle

She's like no one
you've met before
a rare little flower
a precious stone
unpolished, upturned, gritty and growin' up
she's resilient in the shade of adversity
rebellious in the face of a threat
amiable, changeable
you'll like her 'til she
knocks your block off
if you step on her
once cobbled toes
that they stole
that they sold
like her rights from under her stout dipped nose
her sons fought and died
gave their lives
as her daughters heavily bled
in backstreets from dim lit desperate deeds
drugs blackened her teeth
but her spirit, her mind, is blindingly bright
and a beautiful sight to behold
her heart has been broken
bruised, dropped, used up
she's suffered taunts, been ridiculed
and labelled by fools
so when you pick her up
don't patronise her
talk to her
look her straight in the eye
and see her glory blind you sideways, frontways
every bleedin' way

she's a handsome one
but don't drench her in praise
that makes her squirm
beyond her pale confine
let her rise with a pride
that can only be earned
from the life she has given
to all who have lived within her
she's in my blood
she's in my core
she is me
and I am her
she's free, she's a fine thing
but not your thing nor my thing
not a nun nor a moll
between you, me and the wall
that lady taking liberties
she's the belle of the ball.

The Question

Me, I, mine, my
self, inward, reversed eye
from my point of view
from where I stand
the way I see it is
we've all gone blind
blinkered to the
those, them, they, our, us
all searching for the same ubiquitous spirit
through kindred circles unsociable
anti-social mediocrity
likes, bites, blogs, swipes
approves, appraisals, applause
stop, breathe, feel, bond
blend, bend *every* rule
our inner compass facing out
we know . . . we already deep down know
but childlike neediness
grasping at the wrong breast
the wrong neck to smell safe at
leaves us cry alone
so before the aliens come
to give us a sense of community
uncommon humunity
can we forgive if not forget?
Give not to get?
I'll scratch your back first
I'll soften jagged words
my hand is out
don't leave me hanging
If love is the answer
what's the question?

Word Up

Mind. Imagination. Freedom. Flight.
Utopia. Mine. Expression. Right.
Rebel. Blood. Daredevil. Punk.
Relics. Ritual. Comfort. Junk.
Suffocate. Ignorate. Divide. Rule.
Fear. Fight. Repress. Tool.
Educate. Instigate. Integrate. Heal.
Empathy. Rock 'n' roll. Love. Sex. Feel.

The Word Is Out

Do you think of me
when your mind can't breathe
and my blood runs hot
on the cold pale sheets?
Do you?
Do I think of you
when my aching skin
feels fingertips
gliding in?
Do I?!
Did you think of you
when your heartless chest
felt fuck all
ripping mine from my breast?
Did you?
Did you?
I think of you
and your crooked smile
your father's right hand
our unborn child
and your mouth
from out which candied words fell
those moist missed lips
that ate so well
that licked that spit
that spun your spell
the prose the poems
you stole from books
and other's stories
from infidels and conjured up
a killer squirrel
the bird is dead
the word is out.

Miss Nomer

I am not:
a box to be ticked
not a Mrs nor aMiss
my relationship status
is my business
upgrade my title
I'm worth it!

You Don't Get to Be Racist and Irish

You don't get to be racist and Irish
you don't get to be proud of your heritage,
plights and fights for freedom
while kneeling on the neck of another!
You're not entitled to sing songs
of heroes and martyrs
mothers and fathers who cried
as they starved us a famine
or of brave hearted
soft spoken
poets and artists
lined up in a yard
blindfolded and bound
while waiting for Godot
and point blank to sound.
We emigrated
we immigrated
we took refuge
so cannot refuse
when it's our time
to return the favour
land stolen
spirits broken
bodies crushed and swollen
unholy tokens of Christ, nailed to a tree
you hang around your neck
like a noose of the free
our colour pasty
our accents thick
hands like shovels
from mortar and bricklaying
every foundation of cities

you now stand upon
our suffering seeps from every stone
your opportunities arise from
outstanding on the shoulders
of our forefathers and foremothers
who bore your mother's mother.
Our music is for the righteous
our joys have been earned
well-deserved and serve
to remind us to remember
more Blacks
more Dogs
more Irish.
Still labelled leprechauns, Micks, Paddy's, louts
we're shouting to tell you
our land, our laws
are progressively out there
we're in a chrysalis
state of emerging into a new
and more beautiful Eire/era
40 shades better
unanimous in our rainbow vote
we've found our stereotypical pot of gold
and my God it's good.
So join us . . . 'cause
you don't get to be racist and Irish.

The Flower Seller's Daughter

She knows
don't ask
don't fuss
keep quiet
stop goin' on
it'll all blow over

Will it?
Ask her
the flower seller's daughter
she knows.

Black Velvet

Grit-filled nails
salt of the earth
walking o'er streams
running beneath
clopping along
slinking behind
cobbles for irons
non slip of times gone by
that got whipped by the lash of a tongue
and a wind that cut through
auld snappers of heels and hooves
hops roasted on wafts heavenly scent
that I drink as I breathe
dark and deep
sinking then rising
like a rebellious woman
calling me to stand
at her gate
like the saint I'm not
but I do
and I wait
and I wait
and I wait . . .

Poppy

Oh little flower
simple and pure
what have they done to you?
Your blood
that was shed
at the beds
of the dead
fragile and red
in fields once green
now mutated to badges
cheeses and toys
Jesus Christ!
the publicity ploys
and stunts all decoys
while young boys' bones rot
in the ground under pillars
more troops are churned out
to kill not just killers
but people going about their business
shoppers, students
innocents, infants
while legions
take money
and promote recruitments
What have they done to you?
What have they unlearned?
They've cheapened the value
of voices unheard
they changed the banners
and slogans as vets
shout 'Lest we forget!'
But that wasn't it

not what they said
as they limped, bawled
and mentally crawled
out of heavily shelled
holes of hell
to decorated formalities
Remember normality?!
Lest we forget?!
No, little poppet
as you popped your
little head up
from the pools
of blood and muck
if they had a breath left
if they had the strength to stand
you heard them say
'Never again!'

Scent

I washed your robe today
the last traces of you
replaced by a non-biological lavender
I won't lament over anytime soon.
I won't bury my face
deep into the soft synthetic pile
to inhale to the edges of my mind
the musk you left behind
on the collar mostly.

I won't hold it hoping it was you
and wishing its flaccid fabric arms
would wrap around me saying
'I'm here. I've got you babe.
Everything's going to be okay.'
Instead of fallin' limp limbless and empty
leaving me twirling swirling spiralling
headfirst to an unknown terrifying territory
solitary.

Your name won't leave my lips today.
You don't deserve it.
As I wash the last of you away
to the sea.

Irony

Can't think read
write more than this
activism acting up
attacking my brain
flooding my veins
feeling the pain
for the names of those we need to shout about
bang fists on tabletop mountains about
from the African south to the 6 up north
and a million Middle Eastern broken promises
while K West shakes hands with an orange devil
in a House of White
and we pray to our Gods to show us the light
who told us to love, to love not fight
but hands on our ears we magnify fears
and shove books to fuel these man-written rules
down each other's open Munch mouths
as we prance about
in a state of the Tate
while sacred kids' hearts
are ripped right out
and bleed on the Gaza floor
during Birthright tours
So bollocks up yours
I'm doing my thesis
on how shalom means completeness
peace as I'm finding myself
while no fire ceases
and the past
is repeated
  repeated
  repeated.

Dear God . . .

Adore me too
as I am you
there are no others
only us
adorning my head
a crown of gold
riches to covet and curse
and cost us the world
salt of the earth
confine us to crosses we made
while all along
nails we thought strong
rusted and crumbled away
endeavour to break
the binds of a mind
that ignorance blames on fate
hearts that are deaf
to the gods they profess
to love while living in hate
but the gods they *are* us
in us deity
we are the truth and the life
we are the gods and goddesses
we're *not* the sacrifice.

Becoming

I am woman
I am me
mother, daughter, sister, free thinker
activist, writer, boss, singer, sinner
lover, carer, endless beginner
introvert, extrovert, every-kind-of-vert
assertive, confident, confidant
non-conformist, nonchalantly
flaunting, flirting, I'm funny as hell
storyteller, secret keeper
dreamer, reader, non-credence believer
bleeder, bleedin deadly
survivor, thriver, chancer, skiver
I'm a ducker, I'm a diver
I'm hungry for knowledge
but I'm full of it
full of pain, full of joy
one size doesn't fit
like a glove that I'm not
but I am what I am and I'm good with that
I'm ordinary, I'm extraordinary
I'm a queen, I'm a bee
I'm sweetness of honey
I'm salt of the sea
I am the seed
I am the earth
I Gaia, she
I matriarch
I am I
I am we
I am woman
I am me.

BELOW

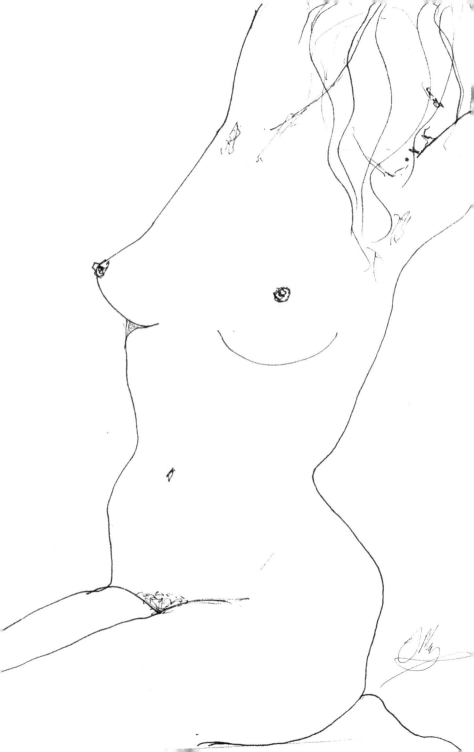

Boom!

That moment you know
it can go either way
a sharp suspicion
split-second decision
loss of contrition
can flip almost everything
a singular kiss
irresistibly blissful
can blow up your world
in a mouth.

Rendez You

You've just gone
I can still taste, smell you,
your masculine scent
on the Shoreditch sheets.

You don't know what you do for me
restore me and my faith in kosher men
decently indecent
deliciously risqué
without deceit, without disdain
without the veil of a game
you don't belong to me
nor I to you

Passing through
one or the other
here or there
not attached but connected
for a while
familiarity evolved
with intermittent intimate flits

I know your kiss
(how your lips feel against mine)
your touch
(the stroke of your hand)
and then
the way you drag me
like a feather pillow
to your side of the bed
plumped, shaped and swathed
in your every limb

Our breath calms, deepens
risen we fall
to a slumberful repose
safe, satisfied
until we meet again.

Smokin'!

A lonesome glow
of a red tip shows
a hidden eye
and I
watch her
watching them . . .

Limbo

Lie back and I'll crouch
slowly, lingering
lower to limbo
downwards to heaven
towards your mouth
insatiously thirsty
salacious and dirty as hell
kneel at my temple
drink from my well
bow, pray, adore, sip
from the cup of Aphrodite
that anticipates your lips.

Slip of a Thing

I could still smell
your sweet scent
on my silk negligée
as I moved through my day
long after your departure
but before you slipped away.

Departure

I left you in
my hotel bed
naked, strong and sweet,
full of drink,
dirty feet and dreams
that make you jump.
Exhaustion hits
as the door clicks closed
my heart misses you already
I'm tired from making love
and mid-turn hugs
when limbs entwined
like vines in the navy night
Warmed to the core
I face the flight ahead.

WTF?

I smoke when I drink
drink when I'm fucked
fuck when I wanna
what the fuck's wrong with that?

The Kiss

Nothing says so much
without a whisper of a word
soft wet blushed lips
part as if tempted
to share a delicious secret
and salivate like juice
of ripened fruit
oozing from the
flesh of the bite
tongues tasting
sweetness of the other
with all the hunger
of a discreet
but starved stranger
surrendering to an eager need
to douse a wolfish greedy nature
I watch his thirst
incline to mine
I feel his breath
fall and rise
as we crave quenching
and oh . . . that rousing moment lips touch
says more than any word could ever hope to.

Ocean

Your heart, humour
hairy chest and chin
lure me in
to fall heels over head
and hand on my heart
I'm terrified
you think when I'm quiet
that I don't feel
if only you knew
(there's an ocean beneath this stream).

Night Stand

Wrap me in your arms
smother me in lust
bury your head between my legs
pleasure to forget
smart my skin alight again
kiss away my ever pain
ripple the sheets tossed and stained
gripped and ripped in someone's name
take me to the edge babe
talk me into bed babe
tempt me, lure me, move me on
from the one whose touch I long for.

Fighting Talk

I have your picture
my vibrator
and high red shoes.

Feathered

The clouds landed
leaving soft white
blankets for
sunsets to lie on
and dreams to sleep in.
I missed their
discreet descent
as I rolled in
a Wilde iron bed
on crisp, white as snow sheets
of sleepless nights
sweat and sweet kisses
with a man of
impure allure
pools for eyes
and a feather
on his back
ready to fly.

Goldilocked Up

You beckon me
from the top of
your tower
I'm scared
still have scars

You beam
seem so sure
I climb
the higher, I know,
the harder the fall
if/when you let me go.

Afterward

We eloped to the shower
where we retangled in oil and water.
Little droplets of
slippery salacious joy
reigniting in
limbs, skin, crevices
we thought we'd left
in the other room.
Steamed, hot, soft, cleaned
you dried me, as you often did.
As I stood conceded,
I kissed your head
whenever it passed
then wrapped it in my breast
as I felt the weight of your thoughts drift away
my fingers circled
the olive tincture deeper
into your aching ears
and I cradled your heavy head
as your neck surrendered
the last of your resistance.

Surrender

Resisting resisting
a beauty conceived
consensual succumbing
accept to concede
attraction entrusted
constraints of control
freedom in losing
relief in letting go.

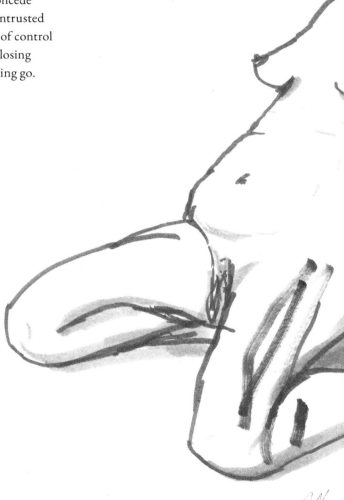

Fiddler's Dance

You saw me in the Fiddler's
and kissed me
I was willing
not when I saw you look me
down and up
in a smoky alley
of leopards and studs
but when I saw you
Look. In. Me.
Your eyes were deep
enough to swim in
so I swam

Did you know
you moved a mind in a feather dress
and a heart on a beat?
Did I know
I swayed a life
in a grilled smile
and a hat full of dreams?
Maybe . . .
so I opened my mouth
and we danced.

Papillon de Nuit

I am the moth
You are the flame
finale hypnotic
conclusion the same

Thrilling the chase
though nothing to gain
pity the hunter
sorrow the game

I show nothing
yet reveal all
you are the puppeteer
I am the doll

My body is willing
my mind hesitates
carnal the knowledge
high are the stakes

Darkness erotic
daylight supreme
I reach for the moon
but you are the dream

When all is too much
and yet not enough
eat me, drink me
delicious the lust

You eat the shoes
that my feet are in
I'll be the food
feasting the sin

Hidden heart races
temple soaked sweat
mouth is a desert
desire is wet

Naked beneath you
weighted with hope
lick me my lover
to my lips from my toes

My lock has been broken
you are the key
chain me, tie me
bind me free

Free from the shackles
of this caged mind
a torrent awaits
as you tighten the blind

Torture brings pleasure
happiness pain
I'll belong to you never
but forever again

So visit me lover
deep in my sleep
forgive me my other
for the deceit

The pen it is mighty
but love is the sword
that cuts like a knife
with every soft word

My heart isn't hollow
it's full to the brim
with joy and with sorrow
I lose and I win

So I fatally flutter
towards your heat
my fate it is sealed
ton papillon de nuit.

I Love to Wake Up with You

The way he walks
the way he laughs
the way his tongue tips
at the mouth of his lips
makes me long to taste
the buds of his sweet
sweltering insatiable lust
and hold my naked honest flesh
in his strong capable
but oh so gentle hands
as the fat of my ass
oozes through his truthful 'want you' grip
and fingers tip
and lovers tiff
and kiss and make out
to make up
and not quite wake up
in that soft focus familiar glow
that burns brighter and longer
than every dawn of any day
I love to wake up with you.

GBH

Grievous battery harm
replaces previous flattery and charm
for readers' wives
whose daily lives
are beyond the hum of the drum
of the washing machine and routine
and so scream at their other halves
for sitting in front of a screen
instead of rollin' in a bed with them
you tube, you porn
KY, new norm
couples solo love
with sock gloves
and 'do not disturb'
on the door down the hall from each other
so, batteries required
to extinguish hot desires
unsatisfied, ungratified
from the bloke who, for a while now,
is umbilically tied
to the strings of his 'the wife' / 'mother of the child'
who he never strokes
as much as the chicken
that he chokes
on his own down the hall
with his Tinder kinder
so, empowered from her
Summer in Siam shazam
and the Summer that is Ann
and the Secrets Victoria gave her
gave her wings and things
that could save her

more than any bull
she's laboured over. Labia Day!
She celebrates over and over
9 times in a row and counting
her wrists get tired
her little rampant boy expires
more batteries required
for her waterproof wand, silver bullets and toys
glittery, gliding, silicone joys
all her wants, wills, filled and thrilled
(no man's tongue
will ever hit *that* spot again)
as she writhes on the vibrations
and the waves of 'sweet Jesus' sensations
as she grievous battery harms herself
all the way
to heaven!

TONGUE

Elephant

There's an elephant in the room
and it's fucking huge
a prophecy of gloom
looming larger than life
of gigantuous height
in full plain sight
and right under our upturned noses
Luca Bos poses
no trumping its trunk
no growling or grunts
it's quiet, big, there
stillness impressive
presence oppressive
passive aggressive
does powerful nothing yet
enough to be felt, smelt
knelt at the alter of
pray, what shall we do?
Call emergency or London Zoo
definitely don't stare
or acknowledge it's there
keep calm and carry on
keep moving along
as though nothing is wrong
make pleasant exchanges
of weatherly changes
'Rain? I say!'
The proper way
stiff upper lip and all that and chit-chat
be a good chap and pass the sugar 'one lump or two?'
But whatever you do
don't mention the elephant
in the room!

Jammy Dodger

He was always
a scaldy child
wasn't he?!
Crusty eyes
scabby lips
flaky bits o' skin
fallin' off of him.

You know the one?
Thingy's son
pink stinky
sticky clammy
jammy bastard
turned into a
handsome fucker
didn't he!

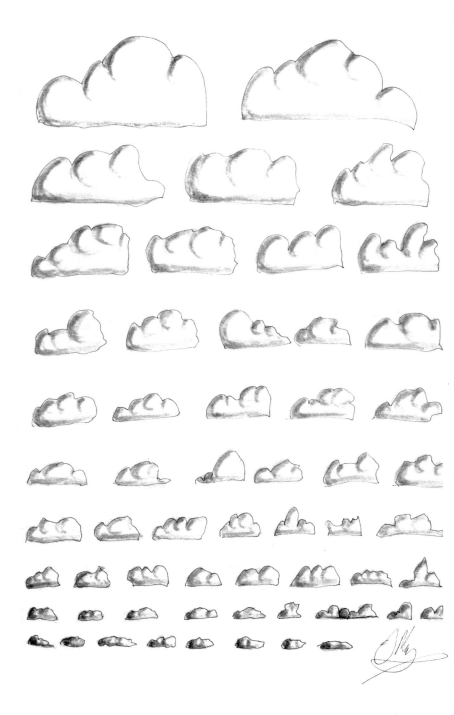

iSmart

iClouds sail by
on my blue iPhone sky
and i wonder why
i can't see them.

Coming Up Roses

Ashes to ashes
dust on a sheet
a load of old rubbish
burned on the heap
when you're breathing you're living
six feet under you're not
a spirit awakened,
compostable rot.
I'm not the body
I habituate in
I'm the mind not the brain
the life that's within
pumping, pulsating
blood through the vein
I'm not the machine
I'm the sun, I'm the rain
that gets under your skin
right under your nose
so until I am not
then I'll be I suppose
in the thing that I live
till I push up the posies
from a pile of manure
life's coming up roses.

Dick

My ex is a dick
egotistical prick
how'd I fall for his shit?
How'd I not see it coming?
Was it love?
Was it lust?
Or concoctions of both?

I sobbed in my sleep
I splintered, I broke
I choked on self-pity
'He hurt me the most'
I've waited for the anger
I knew it would kick in
it's here
it's clear
that prick
is a dick.

It's a Sign

There's a flashing beauty
rusted, roasted
electrically volted
in Nevada's neon boneyard
EXIT.

The Shoot

Mummy didn't hug me
Daddy had to travel
toy guns and nannies
kept me out of trouble.
Today I'm important
rubbing shoulders
slapping backs
mingling through networks
that totally need hacking
ready to pop a small bird
who was bred to not fly
heart races finger braces
horizon in my sight
inadequacies belted up
breath holding in
as 'the help' waves the flag
fooling my ego t'ward me
click bang phew! Got it!
Didn't look a twit
hide my pride behind the eyes
raised higher than my britches
bit of weight upon the leg
I'm hoping to get over
tonight is the night
I might satisfy Leonora.

Prince of Darkness Ditty

Some Anonymous Man
came to call one day
he plundered all the hearts in town
to have his wicked way

His head grew even bigger
than it was when he was born
he walked away without remorse
the saint who had the horn.

Valentine Venom

Roses are dead
violets are too
sugar is toxic
get the hell out of my life.

Sticky Vessel

You have nothing to say
so say it every way
no depth to your wave
no acid to your rave
scratch the surface
crack the paint
off your contoured based face
clouded conceited
louder than needed
to show off
show us
show what?
Your ignorance?
Ignoramus
ignore the anus
peroxidiot, brainless
'cos every thought thinked
out your sticky lips stink.

VIOLET

Eyeballing

Lookin'
not lookin'
look away
look down
look up
look back
don't look
who you lookin' at?!?

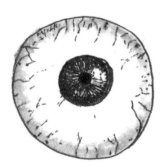

Taking Liberties

Credit where it's due
a halfpenny reflected
bridging a loan
debtors collected
Sinn Féin cornered shops
nuns' sticks got battered
guns rolled in carpets
pushers got busted
by vigils and anties
with prams full of fish
that could fly from pigs
with a sniff of snuff
and a snifter of the black stuff
in a snug, as a dub in a pub
presses 'B' after 'A'
without droppin' the grub
on the moth who's a bird
not a dog that's a weapon
pennies for dinners
each way for winnings
school railings had spikes
to keep out or keep innings
got caught bleedin' rapid
so decades on rosaries
while Joey thumbs stickers
onto tits of the holy
and all you should aim for
other than goals
was not to get pregnant
'til you get on the dole.

Outlook

Towers of clouds
seven hundred feet high
of faces and dogs
fluffy and white
metamorphing into
whatever they like
as ants below
small talk about the weather.

Emergency

Exit   Exit

Fuck you
Fuck the
lot of you.

Exit   Exit

Fowl Play

A flock of birds gathered for the flight of the fancy one
stoking smokes alight for her ascension to new heights
with a poke and a hope to ignite her to life as a wife
with a pocket of glitter and a head full of stars
from Magna Carta to Magnums from Spar
draped in a veil
for ritual thrills
shots from sailors
strippers in frills
black was the eye
smashed as a smile
a neck full of lust
a young guy beguiled
in his nan's at the hands
of a peroxide wild child
dancing queens
messin' around
drowning the laughter
downing the rounds
feathered friendships
comrades cut glass
barefooted bravery
bearing up last
slipping in nipples
bunting and booze
Whitney bewitched
all the single ladies ruled
sure had good craic
for the fabulous friend
she's a good egg
but a wicked hen.

Wofes?

$$\left.\begin{array}{l} \text{woman} - \text{man} = \text{wo} \\ \text{female} \ - \text{male} = \text{fe} \\ \text{Mrs} \quad\ \ - \text{Mr} \ \ = \text{s} \end{array}\right\} = \text{Wofes?}$$

Jog On

Am I a notch on the belt
that holds up your jeans
(just about)?
A dip in an ocean
when you wish for a stream?
Am I a move
in a game I don't play?
A pawn, a piece
to check out with your mates
like the butt of a joke
the lie of a smile?
I am not!
I run a mile.

Fishing

Fishing for a dream
casting into clouds
standing in a stream of thought
running between my toes.

R.I.P.ing the Piss

Death
what a finale
everyone's doing it these days
finishing the chapter
closing the book
going to the next life
covered in muck

I don't care
for the body
we all dance around
the tears are for us
and for our loss
as founders and keepers
lovers and leapers
are lowered into plots
in a pissing well box.

Jesus on the Ceiling

Jesus on the ceiling
where they crucify the song
hanging from each painful note
dying for the end.

EYE

Roses

Who will throw me roses
at the final curtain call?
Who will clap and stamp and chant
in an empty music hall?
I've lived every word I write
and acted up under overlights
but when you go home
arm in arm
I go back to an empty room
no afterglow
after the aftershow
the sacrifice
for art I suppose
it imitates life you see
limitates privacy
I try to give all of me
but hate the cold reality that
lets me live out on the stage
my fantasy when what I really crave
is not 'like' from some
but love from one
so who will throw me roses?

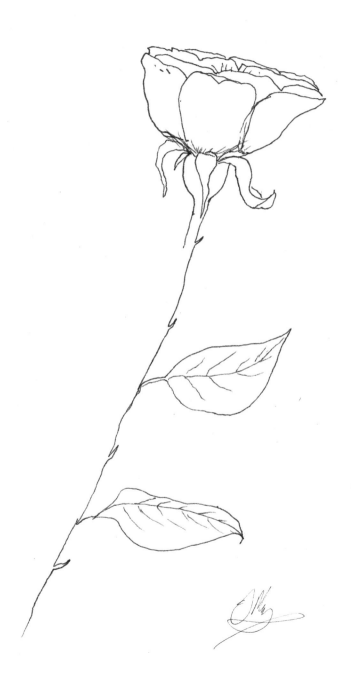

The Last

Is this the last bee
on the tardy rose
on a snappy day
in September?
(Do I wait for another?)

Was that the final swing
skimming the grass
as you squealed and I laughed
more than I ever remember
(you're as tall as your mother)

The damp's in my hair
summer is shut
hoodwinking caps
poke their heads up
but still
I'll wait for
one more . . .

Dubh Linn

Miss her
elegant, intelligent
proud, strong
amazingly graceful
scarred and all
her worn skin
within every dim lit alleyway
her cobbled streets
greet my feet
as I trace
the steps of those beneath
she swims through my blood
like the poddle through hers
the bones of my elders
tangled in her hair
my brother below
cradled in her arms.

Play Date

'I hope you don't mind Mammy
but can you not come?' Ouch!
Simultaneous swell of pride and pain
turns out joy has a sting in its tail

I never saw childhood
from this angle before
from my mother's side
of the lens

I smiled as she skipped
away to play
then I held her hand
a bit tighter.

The Night I Held Your Breath

In out
in out
from the first
incessant, non-stop
regular rhythm
changeable pacemaking
hastening hales
ins and exes
habits escape you
runs away with you
gasp, gulp
hold return
consistently consistent
comforting, catch it
it's running out
I blow mine into yours
it jolts into line
until it doesn't
I held you
as you took your last.

Queen of Fall

The flowers you gave me adorn my kitchen table
stretching their proud
pompom heads
toward the ceiling
their sanguine scent saturates the room
filling my head
drowning my senses
they don't know you've gone
I haven't told them yet.

Blissfully oblivious
they bathe in a vase
a token of your love
that I watched you hold tenuously
at the table
in the 'Puglia of Queen's Park'
the day the leaves turned red
the sound of the cellophane
crackled in your hands
as I walked toward you.

Was it something you thought
you oughta do?
A debutant fulfilling the
obligatory orchid empty promise
for fear of disappointing?

No, I felt it
warm sweet true
your chivalrous flutter
a royal flush
the odds were good
'cause you know I love flowers

I sit here gazing
at them gild
my simple chamber
zealous in their betrayal
unaware
that every time
I look at them
I lose you.

Wide as the World

Before you I am
unguarded, exposed
still bruised from
my previous beatings
(of which there are too many)
but somewhere in me stands
the souls of cold feet
rooted in earth
elevated to greet me
my ancestors' ichor
pours through my veins
my temple pains
with the pulse
of my mothers
womb to womb we grow
Moon Day, De Luian, Gealach we know
to beam in the gloaming
we gleam in the darkest of days
awake!
I call on the spectres that hide in the chorus
we stand on shoulders
as you did before us
and showed a future
that we should look forward to
hiding inside
a cape and crown
this child of a bride
has a soul that is grounded
old as the stones
from which she was founded
and a heart
wide as the world.

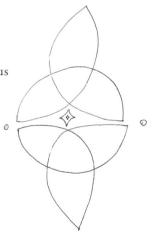

Our Song

Oh how I miss you
how I miss you more now
than ever before
you feel further than miles
and miles from last year
and here is nowhere without you
and yet, my very breath
is a bridge, a naval string
that clings between the divide
a DNA strand of wild
tied up with a satin bow
I wring my hands you held for years
and are yours all over
same veins, same nails and knuckles
no ring could slip o'er without butter
my eyes that cry
to see yours once more
are the mirrors you dived in
times before
when you saw in them
the swell of the sun
and we swam in the glow
and we'd meet at the moon.

Black Eyed and Bashful

She stares right back
black eyed and bashful
from behind a curtain of flame
the left bank of lovers
reflecting in others
Vali renamed in a frame
fringed and infringed upon
sane and unhinged from society
restricting her wild
l'histoire et mémoire
of her dancing in raindrops
a beatnik of shade and light
time will reveal all
one day we'll see her
long after she's gone
long after she's gone.

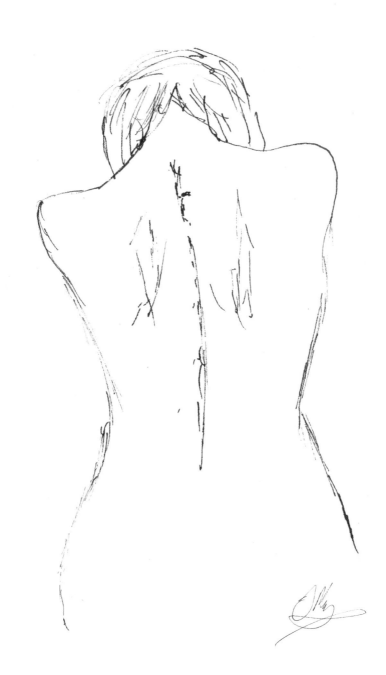

Transition

Contemplate life
observing death
a body in earth
that I've loved, that I love.

A heart floats
in the curve
afraid to land
for fear of flying.

A motion lasts
beyond glass
that separates
'*fin compliquée*'.

I feel more today
than before tomorrow
I love, I envy, I miss
I let go.

Goodnightmare

I lay my head down
on a pillow of regret
turn off the light of hope
tuck myself in for a
night of unrest
as my dreams go up in smoke.

Terminal 2

I went down
    down
    down
    down
    down from the light
on the edge of a cliff
a hell of abyss
held on to the grit
that my fingernails gripped

Crawled on the floor
a dog in the woods
dirt in my hands
grounding in mud

I woke in the lane
I awed at the moon
saw where I was
all alone, all alone

Walked on the bones
in the skin of my feet
those jagged old stones
cut me deep

Not as deep as your words
or the lack of them, boy
when you whistled your way
through an empathic void

Felt alive in the dark
with those sharp little shards
the pain was real
I could feel, I could feel

A physical sense
of my own mortal self
brought my mind back from past
to *this* present tense

Jumped out of a window
away from fear
how quick and how far
could I get from here?

Here? Where?
Here's inside of me
How can I escape myself
to be free?

Oh little white pills
deepen my breath
this beaten heart
deserves a good rest

Good riddance, be gone
this pain in my chest
oh sacred heart
take this nail from my breast

But I can't quite forget
you whistling no tune
as I died then you left me
at Terminal 2.

It's Dawning on Me

'These streets are mine'
said uncle Joe
God rest his soul
as he broke chains
to walk lanes
of his childhood
where the dodder and poddle
twist and twine
underneath shrines
and gods of stone
my bones lie upon
a granite ledge for a bed
under a bitter sky, and I . . .
living the Oscar Wilde dream
'We're all in the gutter
but some of us are . . .'
Some of us are
I'm the ghost on the quiet street
you walk away from
I'm the leaf fallen right through the crack
I'm a creature that loved and lost everything
I'm the clay
only angels can see.

Written for the Simon Community
Influenced by a prelude to 'Raglan Road',
written by Patrick Kavanagh

Mammy's Dying

I dream of her death
wake gasping for breath
then dry sweat
off my soaking skin
the trickles tickle
me to drift again
then I'm 10
and I'm straining to spot her shopping
as the nuns march us up Meath Street
for confessions of nothing.

Then I'm 4
and I'm holding her hand as we walk
and talk and the world is good
and it's sunny
(why is it always sunny?)
and only we know
our secret code
squeeze once I love you
squeeze back I love you too.

Her hands, her hands
that held mine tight
blew kisses goodnight
and swept hair from out of my eyes
how I wish I could crawl
back into her womb
so we could start
all over again.

Waiting

by Tony Clabby

As I look out into the silent glade
I see trees resting bare
the burden of their offspring
reared through summer gone.
The autumn of their lives
scattered beneath,
golden brown.
I feel their warmth upon my soul.
The landscape of my being
mirrored there before me
still and silent
resting.
Waiting for a season coming
whilst evergreens stand guard
silently watching unflinching in the mist.
Waiting! Waiting for birth.
Waiting! Waiting for a new beginning.

TEMPLE

Van Gogh

She danced in the bandstand
at quarter past eight
a doll in a music box
twisting and twirling
dog walkers gawped
'God love her' was thought
as she moved in the silence
of her own space

Oblivious or not caring
of onlooking faces
I envied her will to self-obligate
her execution exquisite
in this open place in the park
she was committed.

A distant red flashed in the green
a phoenix of flame
descended our scene
and circled our singular nut.
Tutued up and ready for the sequence
the leader pressed play
audience receded
and just like that
just like van Gogh
she wasn't mad
she was early.

Pink Moon

The pink moon
would not leave me be
disruptive child
tormented me
to dream of wakefulness
pleading for sleep
unsettling at the blear
where sky meets sea.

B&W

Don't mock me in monotone
when I am a prism.

Thunk

The less I know
the more I learn
the more I learn
I know less than I
thought.

Stay

(05.04.20)

Wake, eat, breathe
wait, watch, sleep away the worry
connect without meeting
missing while seeing your face
on a screen the size of my hand
hoping to see you again
close the door Da
wash the food before
touching the hands
that are cracking like they did
when you painted school railings in the rain
keep safe, stay in
keep going, stay sane
relax, read
do the things
you've been meaning to do
shed the weight
you've been meaning to lose
but not the plot
keep that!
Plant potatoes, dance with the telly
drink the wine you were keeping for 'good'
loosen the clothes
tighten the purse
yoga, piano, cooking
and nothing worse than a whiner
so smile and post that online too.
How about not knowing
what to do for a while
figure it out before
it all goes back to a before

we couldn't keep up with
and keep the good bits
the laughing at ourselves
time with the kids and dog
and neighbours leaving stuff on the step
the bloody good excuse
for not paying the bills
no sweat about not getting dressed
hearing birds again
now the traffic has been turned down
singing songs like you did the first time
music to my ears
that I get from my mam's side
who I miss
while I wake, eat, breathe
wait, watch and sleep away the worry.

Gone Viral

Covid crawled
under my skin last night
my white privileged
thin skin
submersed in brandy
and roll ups
my tongue soured and forked
to a desert palate.

A brimstone head
under a cover of guilt
my dopamine high phone
feeds the low zone
I cried and I cried
like the child
my mother now
thinks I am.

Temples and Bars

Magnificent madness
insobriety brings
dramas delightful
raised volume song sings
crescendos unending
sirens to screams
silence absconded
these Graysonesque queens
chanted and danced threw up
a hail Mary
heeled to cab
greyhounds turn tailing
gulls crying for chips
by gum swapping lips
and the pain doesn't
dampen a thing!

Fact

Freedom's to art
what breath is to life
a box for a mind
is a death of a right.

Celtic Cat

The tiger didn't suit us
all exotic and fierce
we didn't know how
to handle this wild beauty
while trying to tame her
mistaking her for a pet
we hoped to catch and collar
she slinked past
stripes flashed fast
eyes locking ours
she devoured us.

Raven Angel

Bird called to me
crow cawed at me
raven angel
nameless friend
she showed herself
without apology
the spirit of a soldier
sat on my shoulder
talked to me softly
of truth and hope
black as the deepest pool
bright as the reflected moon
upon its surface
she bears the epithet
'prophet of doom'
and so she keeps her cover
from fools and the fears
they eagerly swallow
she hides in night
merging with shadow
she's been hounded, hunted
her family called murderers
tales of her father
at the bust of a goddess.
A poet below
renders nevermore
and laments for the love
of his darling Lenore
but hushly she whispers
of fortune and crosses
capes, crowns
greatness and losses

I listen
her wisdom a gift she departs
as sure as her arrival
she moves down my arm
but before she alights
she squeezes her talon
drawing blood that drops
like a ruby sorrow
crying 'Remember forever
the bird of this feather
said never say never no more.'

Honest to God

Words are prayers
books my bible
tongues, the flames
that fire their survival.

And Finally

When I die
please don't say:
'taken too soon'
'slipped away'
'gone to heaven at last'
'lost', 'sleeping' or 'passed'
'heaven has gained an angel'
'an angel gained its wings'
I'm just dead.
It happens.

Heavy Metal

The snake is for temptation
I accepted then denied
the 1916 windows
for my freedom many died.

The skull is to remind me
I am mortal, I am I
the teardrop to remember
all the ones I didn't cry.

The plectrum for the music
and all the joy it gives
the cross is for a lover
that died so I could live.

The thruppence is the money
that never fully fills
the circle, my child,
and life that never ends.

Firefly

A firefly without fire is a fly.
A night without magic is dark.
Sleep without dreams are forgotten
days without dreams aren't.

Beastly

I met a snake
a sneaky snake
slithered between my legs
filled me with his poisonous junk
and venom in my veins.

I met an ox
strong as a bull
'I'll keep you safe' said he
and chased away all predators
but put the fear of God in me.

I met a squirrel
an ecquriel
relentless in his quest
to crack my nut and down my guard
but pierced my armoured breast.

I met a caterpillar
helped him pupate and fly
he flew so fast
away from me
he never said goodbye.

And so I sit alone.
no more creatures to unrely on
I'm contented with my tiger cub
whose mammy is a lion!

There Was an Old Lady

Poem and drawing by Violet Higham, aged 7

There was an old lady
who was holding the sun
and the sun was holding a hook
and the hook was holding a book
then the book flew away from the hook
and the sun flew into the sky
and left the old lady to die.

Swoop

Poem and drawing by Violet Higham, aged 7

You won't hear
the swoop of a wing
a crack of a stick
or a whisper of a scream
she's the devil
she's a witch
she's the darkness
of the bitch.

The Awakening

by Tony Clabby

Racing, rushing, running, pushing
hurrying, scurrying, can't stop worrying.
My eyes are fixed, my mind is set
things out there that I must get.
Pressure's on, the sweat is dripping
'Oh my God' where is the time slipping?
Bumped old lady pushing trolley
'Excuse me, very very sorry'.
Must keep going, can't hang about
the things I want will be sold out.
Crowds converging, is there room?
My head is spinning, my heart goes boom.
Have not enough, I want lots more
can't have less than those next door.
Stepping swiftly past a gate
saw bulging bundle just too late.
Tripped and staggered then I fell
from the bundle came a yell.
Up it popped a scrawny face
disturbed and sad, so out of place.
So close to much
so far from friend and no warm touch.
There down beside him on the ground
I felt ashamed at what I found.
For I had thought so much of me
the likes of him I did not see.
I have so much I do not need
it must be shared, forgive my greed.

The Calling

It fills my mind with dreams
expanding it to the realms
of stars and beyond
explosive, awakening
pulse pulsating
I chase it
to a place of
weightless agility
galaxious possibility
and an urge I can't control
breath quickens
sweat drippens
logic slippin' away
like a crazed lover
having the hand
yet craving too much more.
Be still you fool.
Compose. Keep cool.
Close your eyes
and surrender
to the calling.

ACKNOWLEDGEMENTS

Thank you so much to all who believe in possibilities and support me in my endeavours, especially in creating this book for you.

Special thanks to:

Ami Cadillac my creative partner of art and magic
Meredith Plant for your endless dedication, vision and work
How did I ever cope without you two?!?
Dee Mulrooney for your transcendent artwork and vibes
Tim Varlow for your beautiful graphic design
Lucy Holliday for your hard work and belief in this project
My manager Craig Logan for your belief in me as an artist
    and your forward vision
Stephanie Mudgett for your endlessly enthusiastic work
Lewis Shaw for socially mediating me
Roddy Doyle for your moving foreword
Lisa Dwan, Bono, Gavin Friday for your guidance
Kathy Scott and Laura Murphy for your teachings
My friends and family for your infinite love and support
My amazing girlfriends for your encouragement and daily joy,
    without you I wouldn't have made this book
Niall for your love and impressive patience during 3am creative ramblings
Violet, your freedom of expression, exuberant creativity, zest for life
    inspires me daily
Mam for your rebellious spirit, determination and love
Dad for introducing me to poetry since time began ˙

Thanks posthumously to:
Uncle Joe for sharing your poems
Auntie Kathleen for spreading your love of great theatre
Padhraig Nolan for opening my ears to know and speak my own words

To you, the reader, for embracing artists and so keeping art alive.
Dip in and out of this book, but always promise to return for more.

Big love, Imelda x

NOTES

NOTES

NOTES